ALL KINDS OF FAMILIES

FAMILIES WITH A
SINGLE PARENT

TANYA DELLACCIO

PowerKiDS
press.

New York

Thank you to my mom, Patty. Everything I am and everything I will become is because of your patience, love, and guidance. I love you to the moon and back.

Published in 2021 by The Rosen Publishing Group, Inc.
29 East 21st Street, New York, NY 10010

First Edition

Editor: Michelle Denton
Book Design: Reann Nye

Photo Credits: Cover DragonImages/iStock/Getty Images Plus/Getty Images; Series Art Vladislav Noseek/Shutterstock.com; p. 5 Dragon Images/Shutterstock.com; p. 7 goodluz/Shutterstock.com; p. 9 Westend61/Getty Images; p. 11 YLightField Studios/Shutterstock.com; p. 13 Jon Ragel/DigitalVision/Getty Images; p. 15 imtmphoto/Shutterstock.com; p. 17 Maskot/getty Images; p. 19 10'000 Hours/DigitalVision/Getty Images; p. 21 Yuganov Konstantin/Shutterstock.com.

Cataloging-in-Publication Data

Names: Dellaccio, Tanya.
Title: Families with a single parent / Tanya Dellaccio.
Description: New York : PowerKids Press, 2021. | Series: All kinds of families | Includes glossary and index.
Identifiers: ISBN 9781725317772 (pbk.) | ISBN 9781725317796 (library bound) | ISBN 9781725317789 (6 pack)
Subjects: LCSH: Single-parent families–Juvenile literature. | Single parents–Juvenile literature. | Children of single parents–Juvenile literature. | Families–Juvenile literature.
Classification: LCC HQ759.915 D45 2021 | DDC 306.85'6–dc23

Manufactured in the United States of America

Some of the images in this book illustrate individuals who are models. The depictions do not imply actual situations or events.

CPSIA Compliance Information: Batch #CSPK20. For Further Information contact Rosen Publishing, New York, New York at 1-800-237-9932.

Find us on

CONTENTS

DIFFERENT FAMILIES

Every child is part of a family, but families come in lots of types and sizes. Some children have families with a mom and dad. Other children have families that are a little different, and that's OK!

Many children grow up in families with just one parent. This could mean a family with just a mom, just a dad, or just a grandparent as **guardian**. These types of families can face a lot of different **challenges**. But they also share a lot of joy and happiness.

The important thing to remember is that even though some families have one parent instead of two, the child is still just as loved and cared for.

5

STARTING OUT SINGLE

There are many kinds of single-parent families, and each one is made from different **circumstances**. Some families start out with a single parent. Adults can choose to adopt a child without a **partner**. Adopted children with one parent are just as loved as every other child.

Sometimes one person in a couple expecting a baby will want to be a parent while the other doesn't. In these cases, a mother or father may choose to raise a child alone.

In 2019, a **census** reported that about 30 percent of children in the United States live in a single-parent household.

7

LOSING A PARENT

Some moms and dads become single parents because of a **tragedy**. When a parent dies, the widow, or remaining parent, is left to care for their family alone.

Everyone **grieves** differently after the loss of a parent. Many things in a person's everyday life, both big and small, will change. People in this position might have a hard time expressing how they feel about all of these changes. They can lean on family to listen and help them get through the hard times.

It might take a little while to get back to the regular **routine** in a family that loses a parent. The remaining parent might ask friends and other family members to help out during the **transition**.

9

FAMILIES OF DIVORCE

Many families have single parents because two parents who were married get **divorced**. When two parents get divorced, they often share custody, or care of, their child or children. After a divorce, some families have two single parents.

Sometimes after two parents get divorced, one parent becomes less involved in the family's day-to-day life, leaving the other parent with full custody. Although it may be hard to see one parent less, children are still loved after a divorce.

Some single-parent families don't include a mom or dad at all. Many children grow up with one of their grandparents. Some children even grow up with an older sibling, or brother or sister, who takes care of them.

TALK IT OUT

No matter what the reason, getting settled into a family with a newly single parent can be hard. If this happens to you, it's important to talk to your parent and other family members about how you feel. It might even help to talk with friends or people at school who have gone through the same thing.

In time, your family will settle into a routine and things will start to feel normal again. It may not be easy at first, but you and your family will get through it together.

Talking to a **counselor** about how you feel about all of these changes can be a big help too!

13

MORE RESPONSIBILITY

Being a part of a single-parent family sometimes means that kids need to have a bit more **responsibility** than other kids their age. A single parent is doing everything alone, and sometimes they might need a little help.

That might mean helping out around the house more with chores such as cooking and cleaning. For kids who are older siblings, it might mean that they need to help watch out for their younger siblings too.

Another way a kid can help out their parent is to make sure they're keeping up with their schoolwork and completing all of their assignments on time without having to be reminded.

15

WORKING HARD

Sometimes single-parent households don't have as much money as other families. Families with two parents may have two incomes, or ways of making money. A family with a single parent only has one income. This can have many different effects on a family's everyday life.

If this is the case with your family, it might mean that you can't go on vacation very often, or that you aren't able to do many extra activities at school. It can also mean that your house or apartment might not be as big or nice.

Single parents work very hard to provide everything they can for their children.

17

MAKING TIME

Some single parents work more than one job to help pay for things like groceries. This might mean some kids with a single parent don't get to see their parent as much as they'd like, or that they spend more time with a babysitter.

If this happens to you, remember that it's just as hard for your parent and they miss you too! If you feel like you aren't seeing your parent enough, try to talk to them about planning an activity to do together each week.

Relationships between children and their single parents can be very close and loving! People in single-parent households often hold a lot of respect for one another, making their emotional bond very strong.

19

NEW RELATIONSHIPS

There may be a time when a single parent starts dating someone or starts spending more time with another adult. All parents need to spend time with their friends sometimes, just like you do! No matter what, it's important to remember that you are the most important thing to them.

Always talk to your parent about how you're feeling, and let them know if you're worried about anything. It might take some time to get to know a new adult in your life, but they will want to get to know you too!

Welcoming a new adult into your family can be challenging. Try to talk to them about the things they like doing—you might have a lot of shared interests!

21

FAMILIES FULL OF LOVE

As relationships change over time, the family members we live with can change too! Even if a family looks different than it once did, or if it seems different from some other people's families, parents still love their kids very much.

Always talk to your parent or guardian about how you're feeling, even if it's hard to talk about. Their biggest goal is to make sure you're happy, safe, and loved!

GLOSSARY

census: A counting of the population done by the government.

challenge: Something that is hard to do.

circumstance: The way things happen.

counselor: A person who provides advice as part of their job

divorce: To legally end a marriage.

grieve: To express sadness for something lost.

guardian: Someone who legally cares for a person.

partner: Someone who works with or is in a relationship with another person.

responsibility: A duty or task you're expected to do.

routine: A regular way of doing things in a particular order.

tragedy: A bad event that causes great sadness.

transition: A passage from one state, stage, or place to another.

INDEX

WEBSITES

Due to the changing nature of Internet links, PowerKids Press has developed an online list of websites related to the subject of this book. This site is updated regularly. Please use this link to access the list: www.powerkidslinks.com/akof/singleparent